Smelly and Terrible Tangles

Damian Harvey

Illustrated by Marijke van Veldhoven

Contents

The Sock-Eater 3

Nelly's Nest 17

OXFORD
UNIVERSITY PRESS

The Sock-Eater

Yan found the thing beneath his bed, sucking a soggy football sock.

He had been looking for his socks for ages. He had looked in the cupboard and on his desk, but there was no sign of the socks anywhere. That meant only one thing ... he would have to look beneath his bed.

Yan shuddered. Who knew what he might find in that terrible place?

He pulled out a plateful of rotten pizza that he had hidden from Mum. The pizza was green and mouldy, and there were hairs growing on the chunks of tomato.

Then he fished out an old pair of trainers. Yan scrunched up his face in disgust. They stank like Dad's favourite cheese.

Yan shone his torch into the dusty shadows, and there it was. It sucked and slurped as if it was eating a chocolate-covered cream doughnut.

'Hey!' cried Yan. 'That's my sock!'

He tried to grab the sock, but the creature swallowed it like a long piece of spaghetti. The sock-eater licked its lips with its fat blue tongue.

'Yum!' it said, reaching for the second sock with its long, thin fingers. Yan snatched the sock as quickly as he could from under the bed.

'You're not having this one,' said Yan, waving the sock above his head.

'Please!' begged the creature. Yan looked into the sock-eater's big round eyes.

'Do you really want it?' asked Yan. The creature nodded and smiled hungrily.

'Well, I suppose
one sock is no use
to anyone,' said Yan.
The sock-eater slurped
it down greedily.

'Yum! Yum!' it said, and
let out a huge burp.

'Cor!' cried Yan, trying to
waft the smell away. 'That really stinks!'

'Stinks!' the sock-eater replied. Then it
yawned and climbed on to Yan's bed.

This is cool, thought Yan. *Just wait until my friends see this.*

Yan had wanted a pet for a long time, but Mum and Dad weren't very keen. He didn't know what sort of creature the sock-eater was, but he knew none of his friends had one. They would be so jealous.

It could eat all the smelly socks in the lost property box at school. He would win first prize in the most peculiar pet competition. It would be so cool.

As Yan walked downstairs, an idea popped into his head and he began to smile.

'Mum?' he asked. 'If I keep my room tidy, can I have a pet?'

Mum and Dad grinned at each other. They knew there was no way Yan would ever keep his room tidy.

'You tidy your room tonight,' said Mum. 'Then we'll see.'

'Yes!' cried Yan as he charged back up the stairs. With a pet like the sock-eater, keeping his room tidy would be simple. Then Yan remembered that he was supposed to be looking for something. 'Mum!' he shouted. 'Where are my socks?'

Mum shook her head in dismay. 'There's a pair down here,' she said.

'Anyone would think you'd been eating them,' said Dad.

'No!' said Yan, turning bright red. 'Not me.'

When he got to school, none of Yan's friends believed his tale about the sock-eater.

'It's probably a dog,' said Josh. 'Our dog eats slippers.'

'It isn't a dog,' said Yan.

'How about a snake?' suggested Allie.

'I think I'd know if there was a snake under my bed,' Yan replied. 'No, it's definitely a sock-eater. You'll see.'

After school, Yan couldn't wait to tidy his room. He grabbed the vacuum cleaner and a duster and went straight upstairs.

'I think he must be serious about wanting a pet,' muttered Dad.

Yan worked all evening on his room. He dusted and polished. He sorted and tidied. He even cleaned under his bed.

While Yan was busy, the sock-eater hid beneath his quilt. When he had finished tidying, Yan offered the sock-eater a new sock, but it didn't seem hungry any more. It looked at Yan's tidy bedroom and pulled a face.

'Yuck!' said the sock-eater in disgust. 'Too tidy.'

When Mum and Dad came upstairs and saw Yan's room, they could hardly believe their eyes.

'It makes ours look like a tip,' said Dad.

'So!' said Mum. 'What sort of pet are you thinking about?'

'This!' said Yan, pulling back his quilt. But there was nothing there.

There was nothing under his bed either, or in the cupboard. Yan searched until bedtime, but the sock-eater had gone.

The next morning, Yan felt miserable without his new pet. He lay in bed and listened as Dad ran up and down the stairs.

'What are you doing?' Mum called.

'Looking for my running socks,' said Dad.

'You're as bad as Yan,' laughed Mum. 'You should put your things away.'

As Dad ran downstairs again, Yan heard something else. A huge grin spread across his face. There was a slurping, sucking sound coming from Mum and Dad's room.

'Yum! Yum!' squeaked a little voice. 'Socks!'

Nelly's Nest

'Have you brushed your hair?' asked Mum.

'Of course,' said Nelly, pulling on her bobble hat.

Dad frowned. 'It doesn't look very brushed to me,' he said.

'I'll do it again when I get to school,' promised Nelly.

Mum shook her head. 'It'll be a right mess when you take that hat off.'

'I'll keep it on all day, then,' grinned Nelly.

Nelly didn't brush her hair when she got to school, and it was too hot for a hat. When she took the hat off, she looked as if she had a porcupine on her head.

'Cool hairstyle, Nelly,' laughed her friends.

'It's the latest fashion,' said Nelly fiercely.

The next morning, Nelly's hair looked worse than ever.

'It looks like a bird's nest,' said Dad. But Nelly didn't care. She hated brushing her hair, so she didn't brush it all that day either. In fact, Nelly didn't brush her hair all week. People started to stare at her as she walked down the street.

On Friday morning, Mum looked sadly at the knots and tangles. 'Please let me do something with it,' she said.

'No!' said Nelly.

As she arrived at school, Nelly felt something small and scratchy land on her head. In the classroom, everyone gathered round to stare, even her teacher, Miss Crumb.

'Why have you got a bird in your hair?' asked Miss Crumb.

Nelly nearly flew to the toilets to look in the mirror. She could hardly believe her eyes.

Bits of straw and leaves had got tangled in the jumbled mass of hair. It really did look like a nest now. And sitting in the middle was a small yellow bird. As Nelly stared at it, the bird cheeped cheekily and started to clean its feathers with its little red beak.

In the playground, all her friends flocked around and peered at the little bird.

'It's cute,' said Chloë.

'I wish I had a bird in my hair,' said Molly. 'My hair is boring.'

Nelly could hardly believe her ears. No one had ever liked her hair before and now everyone was jealous.

When Nelly walked home, a large crowd of people followed her. Some even took photographs. Nelly felt like a movie star as she stopped to smile for the cameras.

Early the next morning, Nelly was woken by the sound of birds singing. Now there were two of them in her hair! The other one must have flown in through the window while she was asleep.

At school, Nelly's hair was soon famous. People kept feeding the birds with bits of biscuit, crisps ... even worms from the playground! And on the way home, Nelly noticed that there were even more people pointing, staring and taking photographs.

For a few days, it was fun. But when the birds woke her up at four o'clock in the morning for the fifth day running, Nelly groaned. She looked in the mirror and pulled a face in disgust. One of the birds was eating a long pink worm and the other was trying to catch a bug that was crawling through her tangled hair.

Nelly thought it might be time to do something about her hair, but Dad helped her decide for certain.

'Look at this,' he said. 'You're famous.'

Nelly stared at his newspaper in horror.

'That's it!' cried Nelly. 'Please do something ... I can't stand it any longer!'

Mum and Dad grinned at each other. Nelly sat in the chair while Mum got some scissors and a comb.

'I'll get the hedge clippers,' laughed Dad, 'just in case.'

Nelly wasn't looking forward to this one bit. But before Mum could start, the front door of their house burst open.

In came a man with a scruffy grey beard and small glasses. He wore a grubby green jacket and wellies. Around his neck was a pair of binoculars. Behind him came a woman with a television camera and a man carrying a big microphone.

'Don't touch a single hair on that girl's head!' demanded the bearded man.

'What?' said Mum, sounding puzzled.

'Those birds are Knobbly Yellow Worm Warts,' said the man. 'They're the only ones left in the world.'

'So?' said Nelly.

'So you can't disturb them until their eggs have hatched and they've all flown away,' explained the man.

'But how long will that take?' asked Nelly.

'Only a few weeks,' said the man. 'But don't worry, they'll be back next year.'

'But they can't come back next year!' cried Nelly.

'Oh yes, they can,' said the man. 'And just to make sure, I'm naming your head as a nature reserve. You must keep it just the way it is.'

Nelly thought she was going to cry. She'd had enough of all this bird nonsense.

However, as the days went by, Nelly began to change her mind. She started to enjoy seeing the birds coming and going with worms and grubs to feed their babies. And when they finally left the nest, she felt a little sad.

Nelly wasn't too upset, though, because she knew they would be back next year. And besides ... she would never have to brush her hair again!

The End

31

About the author

I live in North Wales with my lovely wife, Vicky. I have three wonderful girls, one brilliant boy and a lazy cat called Polly. I've written about 70 books for children and have got ideas for many more ...

I had lots of fun writing the stories in this book. Some people blame the washing machine for missing socks but I couldn't help thinking that it was something else: monsters.

I've never had a bird living in my hair, but my mum used to nag me to brush my hair all the time. She said it looked like a bird's nest. It's hard to imagine that I had lots of hair when I was younger, isn't it?